Steam in the Kitchen

RECIPES WITH A RAILWAY FLAVOUR

Ginny Barnfield

Illustrations & Washing Up
Peter Barnfield

First published 1994
Revised second edition 1999
Revised third edition 2019
© All Copyrights Reserved

No reproduction of any text or illustrations
without written permission of the publishers please

Introduction

Roast Sunday, cold Monday, stew Tuesday, and so on through the endless weeks of a typical post-war English country childhood, then suddenly at nineteen, alone in the city in a small bed-sit, with use of an even smaller kitchen, and a salary smaller still, I discovered that rice didn't just belong in milk puddings, that beans weren't inevitably drowned in tomato sauce, and that survival was possible without meat and two veg. daily.

This early need for economy was the start of a quest for interesting, though not necessarily exotic meals that continues to this day, with a shelf full of cookery books, files of recipes culled from magazines, newspapers, product packets and, best of all, those begged from many friends after enjoying something new and delicious from their kitchens. What follows, therefore, is a dip into the files to give you a taste of some of our favourites which have evolved over the years.

Marrying someone who began by reciting a seemingly endless list of foods he simply would *not* eat did nothing to daunt my enthusiasm, though it certainly exercised my ingenuity. He's eating all of them now, albeit very much disguised, and has loyally tested my culinary inventions for thirty years, emerging from under the endless mountains of washing up to illustrate this small collection with scenes from the Bishop's Teakettle Light Railway, in the County of Whimsey.

The fact that Peter's interest in and enthusiasm for railways has been sustained even longer than mine in cookery (we did, as it happens, meet when I was frying onions for a railway club barbecue) possibly has more than a little to do with the title of this booklet. We hope you will enjoy it. Happy eating!

Ginny Barnfield

Contents

Soups, Salads and Sauces
Porter's Potage 5
Cabside Carrot Soup 6
Sidings Salad 7
Turntable Tomato Sauce 8

Main Courses
Fish-plate Pasta 9
Booking Clerk's Beany Bake 10
Fireman's Fiery Noodles 11
Locomotive Lentils 12
Engine Driver's Egg and Cheese or Tuna Bake 13
Signalman's Sunflower Croustade 14
Ticket Inspector's Toad in the Hole 16
Crossing Keeper's Cabbage 17
Milepost Marrow Rings 18
Ganger's Gingery Millet, Bean Sprouts and Tomatoes 19

Various Puddings
Broad Gauge Dessert 20
Narrow Gauge Dessert 21
Foreman's Fruit Purée and Thick Drink 22
Wheeltapper's Warmer 23
Loading Gauge Pudding 24
Pullman Christmas Pudding 25

Cakes and Biscuits
Guard's Golden Toddy Cake 26
Platform Cake 27
Station Master's Biscuits and Signal Lamp Cakes 28
Ballast Buns 30
Platelayer's Prune and Cheese Scones 31
Freight Train Fruit Loaf 32

Porter's Potage
Potato and Onion Soup

This is a substantial soup, a meal in itself if served with wholemeal bread and garnished with finely chopped parsley or watercress. A good winter warmer, for porters or anyone else who is feeling cold and hungry.

Serves 4 to 6
1lb (400g) potatoes, scrubbed, diced and boiled
2 or 3 medium onions, chopped
2oz (50g) margarine
2oz (50g) flour
About one and a half pints (750ml) liquid, a mixture of the potato cooking water and milk
Salt
Freshly ground black pepper

Melt the margarine in a large non-stick saucepan and fry the onion gently until it is soft but not brown. Stir in the flour, cook for a further 2 minutes, then gradually blend in the liquid, stirring constantly until the soup comes to the boil and thickens. Add the potatoes, cover and simmer gently for 10 minutes, stirring often. Add salt and freshly ground black pepper to taste and serve in warmed bowls.

Variations:
2 teaspoons of yeast extract added with the potato give a completely different flavour but in this case omit the salt. Substitute 2 or 3 sticks of celery for 1 of the onions for a subtle change and garnish with finely chopped celery leaves. For a smoother soup, attack the potato with a masher once it's in the saucepan. For a thinner soup, just add more liquid, or use your thick soup to give some body to a can of "bought" soup. I make a large quantity of the basic recipe, refrigerate any left over and vary it when re-heating. It will not keep for many days without freezing.

Cabside Carrot Soup

The addition of sea salad and spices makes an amazing difference to this apparently simple soup.

Serves 6
2 tablespoons vegetable oil
1 large onion, finely chopped
8oz (200g) carrots, finely chopped or coarsely grated
1 cup sea salad, dried
3oz (75g) red lentils
1 teaspoon cinnamon
1 teaspoon freshly grated nutmeg
1 teaspoon dried marjoram
Two and a half pints (1250ml) stock or water

Heat the oil in a large saucepan and allow the vegetables to sweat over a low heat with the lid on for 15 minutes, stirring occasionally. Add the lentils, sea salad, spices, marjoram and water or stock, bring to the boil whilst stirring, cover and simmer for 20 minutes. I usually speed things up by using a kettle of boiling water. Cool slightly before liquidising, reheat and serve with freshly ground black pepper.

While the soup is cooking, split and butter some soft wholemeal rolls, wrap them in foil and heat through in a medium oven, warming some plates and bowls at the same time. This is a fairly thin soup so do be generous with the bread.

Sidings Salad

A bowl of salad accompanies most of our main meals, but what about the time when there's not a tomato, lettuce leaf or slice of cucumber in the house? Here are some ideas.

3 or 4 tablespoons plain yoghurt
1 large carrot, peeled and chopped
1 large Bramley or 2 dessert apples, peeled and chopped

Purée in a blender with enough orange juice or water to give a virtually fat free dressing for whatever is available from this list:
White or red cabbage or Chinese leaves, finely shredded
Celery, red, yellow or green pepper, finely chopped
Button mushrooms, quartered or thinly sliced
Frozen peas, soaked 5 minutes in boiling water
Cooked beetroot. Use as garnish if you don't want pink salad!
Canned sweetcorn, beans or chick peas
Nectarine, peach, orange or kiwi fruit, peeled and chopped
Raisins, sultanas, apricots, prunes. Use straight from the packet or soak in boiling water for a softer texture if preferred.
Sunflower or pumpkin seeds, nuts of any kind. Peanuts dry roasted for 10-15 mins. Gas 5, 375 deg F, 190 deg C are great. (I keep a jar handy for instant energy during the day).
Bean sprouts, or other sprouted seeds. Grow your own on the kitchen window sill with an inexpensive sprouter: sow beans or seeds in the stacking trays, water daily and harvest a few days later. It's that simple! Our favourites are alfalfa and green lentils.

Serve in individual bowls with a colourful garnish: sweetcorn and red cabbage, peas and red pepper, apricots and prunes, pumpkin seeds and raisins all look great. Let your imagination run riot, and do remember to provide spoons for those elusive bits at the bottom of the bowl! On really hot days a generous bowlful, with perhaps a little diced cheese and thinly sliced bread and butter, makes a meal.

Turntable Tomato Sauce

2 or 3 onions, finely chopped
3 or 4 cloves garlic, chopped
2 tablespoons vegetable oil
400g can tomatoes
2 to 4 teaspoons cornflour
1 tablespoon tomato or vegetable purée
Salt and freshly ground black pepper
1 teaspoon mixed herbs - oregano, thyme, parsley, basil, sage
OR a pinch of cayenne pepper (good on nut roasts, falafels etc.)

Fry onion and garlic gently in the vegetable oil in a covered saucepan until soft but not brown. Mix the cornflour to a smooth paste with the juice from the tomatoes and add to the pan with the tomatoes, roughly chopped, the herbs and seasoning. Boil, stirring constantly, until thickened, then add tomato purée dissolved in a cup of boiling water. Continue to cook, stirring, and adding more boiling water until the sauce is the thickness you need. (Thick sauce takes up less room and you can thin it down later! I always make extra as it's such a versatile basic to have handy in the fridge).
This is *the* sauce to accompany any kind of pasta. Make it very thin for cannelloni, which absorb a great deal of liquid. For a simple, quick "mock pizza" for 2, use:

6oz (150g) self raising flour, 50/50 white/wholemeal
2 tablespoons vegetable oil
Pinch of salt
A little water to mix

Mix to a soft dough, roll out on a floured baking sheet and pinch up the sides. Spread with pesto if you like it, or simply cover with thick tomato sauce right out to the edges and top with sliced or grated cheese. Bake for 20 minutes in a pre-heated oven, Gas 6, 400 deg F, 200 deg C. Serve with plenty of salad - coleslaw is particularly good with this dish.

Fish-plate Pasta

Here's a quick, simple dish, just right after a day working out on the line. *(Fishplates are the metal plates used in pairs to join lengths of railway line together. They need removing and oiling regularly).*

Serves 4
Turntable Tomato Sauce (see page 8)
6oz (150g) wholemeal pasta, any kind
Canned or smoked fish e.g. mackerel, pilchard, tuna
2oz (50g) margarine
2oz (50g) plain flour
1 pint (500ml) milk and pasta cooking water, 50/50
Freshly ground black pepper
2oz (50g) tasty cheese, grated

Grease 4 oven-to-table bowls and put a generous dollop of tomato sauce in each, together with a helping of fish. Cook the pasta, strain, reserving the cooking water, and divide between the bowls, mixing well. Melt the margarine, add flour, cook for two minutes, then gradually add the milk and water and bring to the boil, stirring constantly until the sauce thickens. Season and pour over the bowls, sprinkle with the cheese and bake for 30 minutes, Gas 5, 375 deg F, 190 deg C. Brown under the grill for a few seconds for a crisp top and serve with a green salad, orange slices and lemon wedges.

Booking Clerk's Beany Bake

This quick and easy dish relies on ready cooked mashed potato and vegetarian sausages or burgers, so remember to cook extra when you have bangers and mash. Alternatively, use Smokey Snaps or Bacos (bacon flavoured soya chips).

Serves 2
1 tablespoon vegetable oil
2 onions, chopped
2 cloves garlic, chopped
400g can baked beans in tomato sauce
1 teaspoon dried or 1 tablespoon fresh sage
2 tomatoes, quartered
2 cooked sausages, burger or soya chips
1lb (400g) mashed potato

Fry the onion and garlic gently in oil until soft, add beans and sage, divide between two lightly greased or oiled oven-to-table bowls. Add chopped sausage, burger, or a helping of soya chips, plus the tomatoes, and cover each bowl with a layer of mashed potato. Make furrows with a fork, dot with margarine and bake in a moderate oven, Gas 5, 375 deg F, 190 deg C for about 30 minutes. Brown under a pre-heated grill for a few seconds for a crisp top.

Variation:
Use 4oz (100g) wholemeal self-raising flour instead of half the potato, add a beaten egg (reserve a little to glaze the top) and a teaspoon of mixed herbs or chopped fresh rosemary, thyme, oregano, whatever you have available. Spread this mixture over the bowls, brush on the remaining egg and sprinkle with sunflower or sesame seeds for a crunchy top.

Fireman's Fiery Noodles

Serves 4
2 tablespoons vegetable oil
1 bunch spring onions, sliced
1 head calabrese, broken into florets
A few small mushrooms
1 red pepper, deseeded and sliced
3 or 4 tomatoes, quartered
1 inch fresh ginger, grated (Freeze it for easy grating)
1 227g can water chestnuts, sliced
1 cup sea salad, dried
150g pkt. marinated tofu pieces
1 tablespoon vegetable purée
6oz (150g) wholemeal noodles

In a large saucepan or skillet gently stir fry the onions, ginger, calabrese, mushrooms, red pepper and tomatoes. Cover and cook until just tender. Meanwhile, pour hot water on the sea salad to fill the cup and dissolve the vegetable purée in another cup of hot water. Add both to the vegetables, plus the sliced chestnuts and tofu, stirring gently to avoid breaking up the calabrese. Put 4 lightly oiled bowls to warm in a low oven, quickly cook noodles as directed, strain and divide between the bowls and pile the vegetables on top. This combination of green and red, soft and crunchy, looks attractive and tastes superb.

Locomotive Lentils
Dhall

A versatile dish to serve with rice, poppadums, parathas or puris, and chutney, raita or a tomato sambal.

Serves 4
8oz (200g) red lentils
2 tablespoons vegetable oil
2 onions, chopped
2 to 4 cloves garlic, chopped
1 to 2 teaspoons each of ground cumin, coriander and turmeric
(Omit one of these three altogether for a complete change of flavour)
2 good pinches each of cayenne pepper and fenugreek
2 tablespoons vinegar - malt, wine or cider
2 tablespoons tomato purée mixed with 6 tablespoons water
Salt to taste

Cook the lentils with 1pt (500ml) water in a large covered pan until like thick porridge. N.B. Watch them - they *will* boil over! In another pan, fry the onions and garlic gently in oil until soft, add the ground spices mixed to a paste with the vinegar and cook 2 or 3 minutes more. Add cooked lentils, tomato purée and salt to taste.

Variations:
Use any left over dhall to fill pasties, adding chopped apple, sliced tomato or onion rings for extra flavour and moisture. It's very good in pancakes too. In this case you could leave out the tomato purée and water, to give a stiffer mixture, and serve the pancakes with Turntable Tomato Sauce (see page 8), substituting cardamom, cloves, cinnamon and cayenne for the herbs.

Accompaniments:
Raita: Natural yoghurt, finely chopped cucumber and fresh mint.
Sambal: Finely chopped tomato and onion, dessicated coconut and lime or lemon juice.

Engine Driver's Egg & Cheese Bake

Serves 2
2 large onions, chopped small
2 tablespoons vegetable oil
4 eggs
4oz (100g) wholemeal breadcrumbs
3 tomatoes, halved or quartered if large
2 tablespoons fresh herbs e.g. sage, parsley, oregano
Half a teaspoon mustard
Freshly ground black pepper
2oz (50g) tasty cheese, grated

Heat the oven to Gas 8, 450 deg F, 230 deg C and line a 7 by 11 inch tin with baking parchment. Fry the onions gently in the oil until soft. Beat the eggs lightly in a large bowl, add breadcrumbs, herbs (use dried if you have nothing fresh available), mustard, pepper and half the cheese. Add the cooked onions, mix well and spread evenly in the tin. Push the tomatoes down into the mixture with cut sides uppermost and sprinkle the remaining cheese on top. Bake for about 20 minutes and serve with a green salad.

Variation:
Omit cheese, mustard, sage and oregano. Use just one onion, 2 eggs, and a small can of tuna flakes. Be generous with the parsley.

Signalman's Sunflower Croustade

This signalman has a herb garden, but you can of course use dried herbs if fresh ones are simply not available.

Serves 4
6oz (150g) wholemeal breadcrumbs
2oz (50g) sunflower seeds
2oz (50g) sesame seeds
2oz (50g) cheese, grated
2oz (50g) soft margarine
1 clove garlic, crushed or finely chopped
1 teaspoonful each of fresh basil, rosemary and oregano

Mix all the above ingredients well together with a fork and press firmly into the base of an 8 inch loose bottomed cake tin lined with baking parchment. Bake for 20 minutes, Gas 4, 350 deg F, 180 deg C.

For the sauce:
2oz (50g) margarine
2 medium onions, finely chopped
1oz (25g) plain flour
10fl.oz (250ml) milk
2 large tomatoes, chopped
2 tablespoons sage, chopped
Salt and freshly ground black pepper

Fry onions gently in margarine till soft, add flour, cook two minutes more, add milk gradually, stirring until thick, then add tomatoes, sage and seasoning. Pour over the cooked croustade and bake for a further 20 minutes. This is very good served with peas (frozen or young fresh) cooked gently in butter with some finely shredded onion, 2 or 3 outer lettuce leaves, a little salt, sugar, black pepper and 2 large sprigs of mint, but a green salad will do equally well if you prefer it.

Ticket Inspector's Toad in the Hole

Use your favourite vegetarian sausage meat or sausage mix for this variation on a traditional English dish.

Serves 2
4oz (100g) plain flour
Pinch salt
1 egg
About half a pint (250ml) milk and water
1 tablespoon vegetable oil
8oz (200g) sausage meat, shaped into 8 flat rounds
2 medium onions, sliced in rings
1 large cooking apple, peeled and chopped

Mix the flour, salt, egg, milk and water to a batter.
Preheat the oven to Gas 7, 425 deg F, 220 deg C and heat the oil in a large roasting tin.
Put the sausage meat in the tin, top each round with an onion ring, fill the spaces with the chopped apple and any remaining onion, pour the batter over and bake for about 30 minutes. This is particularly good served with **Crossing Keeper's Cabbage**, which offsets the richness of the sausage meat very well.

Crossing Keeper's Cabbage

Gardening was a traditional occupation for the crossing keeper, with his (or her) cottage alongside the line, so this could be a virtually home grown dish.

Serves 4 to 6
1 small red cabbage, thinly sliced
12 small onions, peeled
2 or 3 cooking apples, peeled and chopped
4 to 6 tablespoons vinegar - cider, wine or malt
About a pint (500ml) water
Freshly grated nutmeg, to taste
Pinch of salt
1 tablespoon soft brown sugar

Put half the liquid and all ingredients except the sugar in a large covered saucepan and stew gently for 1 hour or until tender (or pressure cook for 10-15 mins). Add the sugar with the remaining liquid and boil, stirring, to reduce to a thin syrupy consistency. Any left overs will keep well in the fridge.

Variations:
Substitute a tablespoon of caraway seeds for the nutmeg to give a subtly different flavour, or simply omit the spice altogether.

Milepost Marrow Rings

Serves 2
2 tablespoons vegetable oil
4 marrow rings, an inch thick, peeled and deseeded
1 medium onion, finely chopped
4oz (100g) carrots, coarsely grated
1 teaspoon cumin seeds
Half a teaspoon each of paprika and turmeric
4oz (100g) creamed coconut, grated

Heat one tablespoon of oil in a large roasting tin in a fairly hot oven Gas 6, 400 deg F, 200 deg C. Place the marrow rings in the tin, turning once so that each flat surface has a thin coating of oil. Fry the onions gently in the remaining oil, add carrots and spices, cook 5 minutes more, stirring frequently, then remove from the heat and stir in the coconut. Divide this mixture between the marrow rings, return to the oven and cook for a further 45 minutes to an hour, depending on the size and age of the marrow. Alternatively, use 2 or 3 courgettes, split lengthwise, the flesh scooped out carefully with a teaspoon so as not to break the outer skin and added to the stuffing mixture. In this case, roast for the shorter time. This is a rich dish, best served with plain boiled diced potatoes, very low fat yoghurt and lots of finely chopped fresh mint.

Ganger's Gingery Millet with Bean Sprouts and Tomatoes

I thought of millet as food for budgerigars until I found this quick and easy recipe, guaranteed to warm up the coldest worker.
(The ganger supervises a group of men who maintain or repair the track).

Serves 4
1 tablespoon vegetable oil
2 onions, chopped
2 cloves garlic, finely chopped
1 inch fresh ginger, grated (Freeze it for easy grating)
8oz (200g) millet
1 pint (500ml) boiling water or stock
A good pinch of salt and freshly ground black pepper

Fry onion, garlic and ginger gently in oil until soft, add millet, seasoning, and liquid. Boil, cover and simmer for 30 minutes, when the liquid will be absorbed. Turn off the heat, wait 5 minutes, fluff up with a fork and serve topped with the following:

1 tablespoon vegetable oil
4 to 6 cloves garlic and 1 or 2 onions, finely chopped
1 teaspoon fresh ginger, grated
1 or 2 green chillies, deseeded and finely chopped
OR 2 good pinches of chilli powder or cayenne pepper
1 heaped teaspoon coriander
2 tablespoons vinegar and a pinch of salt
2 or 3 tomatoes, fresh or canned
1 packet beansprouts
Peanuts, fried, or marinated tofu, sliced and fried until crisp

Stir-fry the vegetables rapidly in the oil at full heat, add spices and vinegar, and the beansprouts last of all. Sprinkle the peanuts or tofu on top and serve quickly.

Broad Gauge Dessert

I'm afraid this is not good for waistlines!

Serves 2
1 banana, mashed
2 dessert apples, grated
2 tablespoons raisins
2 digestve biscuits, crumbled
Rich and creamy yoghurt for topping

Mix together, divide into two glasses, top with a generous helping of yoghurt and serve immediately so that the biscuits stay crisp.

Narrow Gauge Dessert

You can enjoy this one and not feel guilty!

Serves 2
1 banana mashed with 2 tablespoons low fat yoghurt
1 dessert apple, grated
1 orange, peeled and chopped
1 kiwi fruit, halved, fruit scooped out and chopped
Natural low fat yoghurt or fromage frais for topping

Put banana mixture (using a blender for a smoother texture if you prefer) in the base of each glass, add the rest of the fruit in layers.

Foreman's Fruit Purée

Serves 2
4 soaked ready-to-eat prunes
2 dessert apples, peeled and diced
6 tablespoons stewed apricots and juice
4 apricot halves

Put 2 chopped prunes in the bottom of each glass. Purée the apples and stewed apricots with their juice in a blender and pour over the prunes. Decorate with the apricot halves and pour on a little yoghurt, fromage frais, cream or cream substitute if you wish.

Variations:
Stewed plums instead of apricots give a wonderfully pink dessert. Use 3 apples and the juice of a large orange *or* 2 bananas and 4 tablespoons low fat yoghurt for the purée, topping with kiwi fruit or strawberries. You will soon be adding your own ideas, I'm sure.

Thick Drink

This super refreshing drink evolved from our fruit purée desserts.

Fresh apricots, stewed in a little water
Natural low fat yoghurt
Apricot and grape juice

Simply put in the blender roughly equal proportions of fruit, yoghurt and juice, mix really well, pour into small glasses and serve immediately. For a longer drink, pour into tall glasses and add mineral water, still or sparkling according to your taste. To enjoy the natural sweetness of the fruit, leave out the juice, using water instead. Although quite sharp, this is an even more refreshing version and excellent in a heatwave!

Wheeltapper's Warmer

This hot fruit salad is wonderfully comforting on a cold day and as it keeps well in the fridge I usually make double the quantity.
Once a familiar sight and sound at major railway stations, the wheel tapper used to walk along trains striking each wheel with a long-handled hammer and listening for the change of tone which could denote a defective wheel.

Serves 2
4 prunes, pitted
4 apricots, dried
2 tablespoons Lexia or muscatel raisins
1 firm banana, thickly sliced
1 dessert apple (Cox's Orange Pippin for flavour!), diced
A good pinch of cinnamon or mixed spice

Put all the ingredients in a small saucepan with just enough water to cover. Bring to the boil, simmer 15 minutes, remove from the heat and allow to stand for at least 30 minutes for the flavours to blend. Re-heat to serve but do be careful: scalding hot fruit is painful! Top with a little yoghurt, fromage frais or single cream if you wish.

Loading Gauge Pudding

Wagons piled high with this pudding will satisfy the heartiest appetite. It's a luxury version of that good old fashioned stand-by, bread pudding, and is equally good hot or cold.

8oz (200g) stale bread, including crusts
2oz (50g) soft margarine
2oz (50g) sugar
1 egg
1 tablespoon marmalade
4oz (100g) curants, raisins or sultanas
2oz (50g) dried apricots, chopped
2oz (50g) dried prunes, chopped
1 teaspoon mixed spice
Nutmeg, freshly grated, to taste
Grated rind of one lemon, scrubbed to remove wax
Milk to mix
1oz (25g) Brazil nuts, chopped

Break the bread into small pieces, soak half an hour in cold water, drain and squeeze as dry as possible. Cream the margarine and sugar in a large mixing bowl, then add the egg, marmalade, fruit, spices, lemon rind and bread. Mix thoroughly, with enough milk to give a soft dropping consistency, and turn into a tin well greased or lined with baking parchment. Spread evenly, pressing down with a fork, scatter the Brazil nuts over the top, pressing them gently into the mixture, and bake for about an hour, Gas 3, 325 deg F, 170 deg C.

Pullman Christmas Pudding

For speed and luxury this pudding takes some beating. It is much lighter than many versions and needs no maturing, so you can leave making it right up to Christmas Eve if necessary!

Serves 6 to 8
4oz (100g) Demerara sugar
3oz (75g) soft margarine
8oz (200g) raisins
8oz (200g) sultanas
2oz (50g) candied peel
6oz (150g) fresh wholemeal breadcrumbs
Grated rind and juice of 1 lemon (scrub well to remove wax)
1 teaspoon almond essence
Half a teaspoon each of nutmeg, cinnamon and mixed spice
2 eggs
3 tablespoons milk
1 tablespoon brandy

Cream the sugar and margarine, add breadcrumbs, fruit, peel and spices, beaten eggs, milk and brandy. Mix very thoroughly, giving everyone a stir for luck! Steam for 4 hours in a greased 2 pint (1 litre) basin, and for a further 1 hour on the day itself. Serve with rich and creamy yoghurt, your favourite sauce, or simply single cream.

Guard's Golden Toddy Cake

This wickedly simple cake is soaked in whisky syrup as it comes from the oven and certainly needs to be well guarded!

5oz (125g) margarine
4oz (100g) soft light brown sugar
6oz (150g) clear honey
1 tablespoon water
2 eggs
7oz (175g) self raising flour
2oz (50g) white sugar
1 tablespoon whisky (or more, to your taste!)

Heat the oven to Gas Mark 4, 350 deg F, 180 deg C. Gently melt the margarine, brown sugar, honey and water in a saucepan, cool slightly, beat in the eggs, sift in the flour and beat to a smooth batter. Pour into a 7 by 11 inch tin lined with baking parchment and bake for 30 to 35 minutes until springy to touch.

For the syrup, dissolve the white sugar in 3 fl. oz (85ml) water in a small saucepan, boil for 5 minutes and remove from the heat. Add the whisky and pour the warm syrup over the cake as it comes from the oven, after first pricking the surface with a fork. Allow to cool completely before removing from the tin.

Platform Cake
No-bake Chocolate Cake

Most cooks have their own version of this ever-popular biscuit cake. This one uses plenty of cocoa to give a really bitter chocolate taste.

4oz (100g) hard margarine
2oz (50g) soft brown sugar
2oz (50g) sultanas or raisins
3 tablespoons cocoa
1 egg, beaten
7oz (175g) digestive biscuits

Crush the biscuits to fine crumbs - a tough polythene bag, twist-it and rolling pin make this easier, or, if there are children in the house, you might even let them stamp on the bag, gently of course!

Melt the margarine in a saucepan with the sugar, add fruit, cocoa and beaten egg. Bring to the boil, remove from heat and add the crushed biscuits, mixing thoroughly. Press into a 7 inch square tin lined with baking parchment and when cool, refrigerate until firm.

We find this cake quite rich without any topping but if you are feeling really wicked and indulgent, you could always melt a few squares of dark cooking chocolate and put a blob on each piece!

Stationmaster's Biscuits

Long slow cooking gives these golden oat biscuits their essential crispness. They keep well so I try to make a huge batch before Christmas - they make an attractive gift in a glass jar. Use half the following quantities if you just want enough for home consumption!

1lb (400g) margarine
4 tablespoons golden syrup
1lb (400g) plain flour
3 teaspoons bicarbonate of soda
10oz (250g) porridge oats
8oz (200g) sugar

In a large saucepan gently melt the margarine and syrup, then add all the dry ingredients and mix very thoroughly together. Roll into small walnut sized balls, place on greased baking trays and bake for approximately 2 hours, till golden brown, in a very cool oven, Gas 1, 290 deg F, 150 deg C.

Signal Lamp Cakes

Decorate these delicious little melt-in-your-mouth cakes with jam or angelica, depending on whether you want to signal STOP or GO!

4oz (100g) margarine
1oz (25g) icing sugar
1 or 2 drops vanilla essence
4oz (100g) self raising flour
Red jam and angelica or lime marmalade

Cream the margarine and sugar, add vanilla essence and sift in the flour. Mix well with a fork, divide into 18 small balls, flatten slightly and make a slight hollow in the centre of each for the jam.

Preheat the oven to Gas 5, 375 deg F, 190 deg C and bake in paper cases for 10 to 15 minutes. Dredge with icing sugar and pop a dollop of red jam or a piece of angelica in the centre of each cake. If you don't like angelica's distinctive flavour, lime marmalade will do just as well and will certainly make a more appropriate shape!

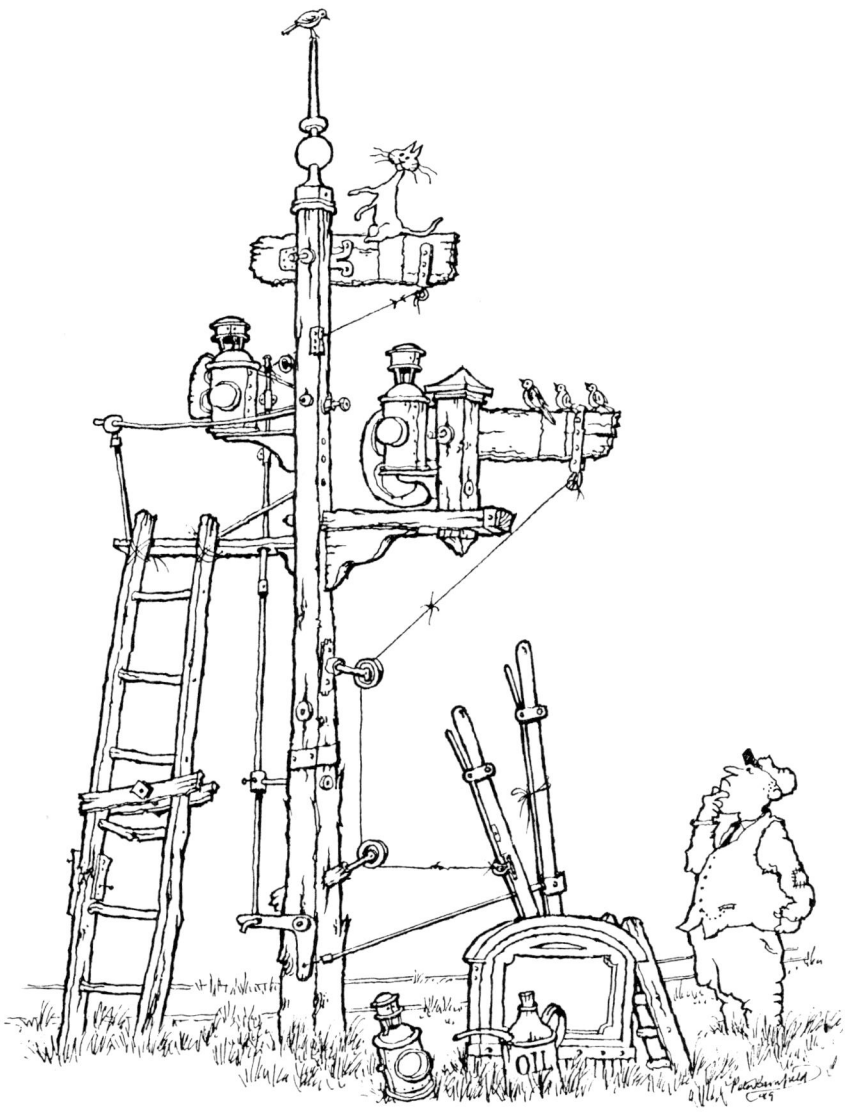

Ballast Buns

These are indeed rock cakes!

In railway terms, ballast is the stone on which the actual track is laid. It looks like giant-sized gravel.

4oz (100g) margarine
8oz (200g) self raising flour
4oz (100g) soft brown sugar
4oz (100g) currants or mixed fruit
1oz (25g) glacé cherries, chopped
Grated rind of one lemon (scrub well to remove wax)
Nutmeg, freshly grated, to taste - up to half a teaspoon
1 egg, plus a little milk if necessary

Preheat the oven to Gas 6, 400 deg F, 200 deg C. Rub the margarine into the flour until crumbly and add all the remaining ingredients. The mixture should be fairly stiff. Spoon onto a baking sheet, greased or lined with baking parchment, in 10 or 12 rough heaps and bake for 15 minutes.

Platelayer's Prune & Cheese Scones

This may sound an odd combination, but it works really well, the fruit keeping the scones moist enough to be edible the next day, if there are any left, of course! *(A platelayer works on the railway track. The term dates back to the very earliest plateways).*

8oz (200g) wholemeal self raising flour
1 teaspoon baking powder
1 teaspoon mustard powder
Pinch of salt
2oz (50g) soft margarine or sunflower spread
1oz (25g) cheese, grated
2oz (50g) ready-to-eat prunes, chopped
Quarter pint (125ml) milk

Heat the oven to Gas 8, 450 deg F, 230 deg C. Mix all the ingredients quickly with a fork, using just enough milk for a soft dough. Wholemeal flours vary in the amount of liquid they absorb, but if your dough is too slack just use plenty of self raising flour to roll it out to about an inch thick. Using a metal cutter to slice through the prunes, cut into rounds of whatever size you prefer: tiny ones for a dainty buffet, largest size for a hearty lunch. Place on a greased or non-stick baking sheet and bake for 8 to 10 minutes. Cool on a wire rack, split and serve spread with soft cream cheese.

Freight Train Fruit Loaf

Here's a quick easy-to-make loaf to sustain the crew of the slowest goods train. It's very sticky and equally good eaten warm, as a pudding! Quantities are for 2 one-pound loaf tins.

Half pint (250ml) water
6oz (150g) sultanas
8oz (200g) dark brown sugar
7oz (175g) margarine
2 teaspoons bicarbonate of soda

In a large non-stick saucepan boil the above ingredients over medium heat for 10 minutes. Watch it carefully or it will froth up and boil over! Cool the mixture down and add:

12oz (300g) wholemeal plain flour
2 eggs
2 teaspoons baking powder

Mix well together, divide between two tins lined with baking parchment and bake at Gas 5, 375 deg F, 190 deg C, for 90 minutes.